The Game of Politics: The Cardinal Sins of The Liberal Party of Canada in 2019

W.L. SEATON

TEAZER
PUBLISHING
February 2020

The Game of Politics - Board Game

The Monopoly type board game on the cover was created by my close friend Leonard Giffen, and designed and printed by me in Halifax in 1975. Len's knowledge of the game of politics was extensive when Pierre Elliott Trudeau was Prime Minister. Len and I have spent a good portion of our adult lives in and around politics, therefore we can write about **"The Game of Politics"** knowing it's in our DNA and more than just a board game.

The table of contents has stories on my personal involvement in T**he Game of Politics** with the balance of the book my assessment of **The Cardinal Sins of the Liberal Party of Canada in 2019.**

I am writing about my life as a long time Liberal and my personal experiences relating to the Liberal Party as a supporter and a Provincial candidate. The seed for this book came partly from my knowledge and perceived knowledge about **The Game of Politics.**

DISCLAIMER: A lot of what I write about happened decades ago and is from my memory and may not be totally correct. (*I plead the fifth and refuse to answer any questions, especially on the grounds that I might incriminate myself*).

Most of the more prominent names I have mentioned have passed on to some political party in Heaven or Hell. I refrain from stating which party they belong to.

CONTENTS

Liberal riding of Notre-Dame-de-Grâce

Warren Allmand

My entry into politics was supporting Liberal candidate William Warren Allmand in his Montreal riding of Notre-Dame-de-Grâce in 1968. Warren served in the cabinet of Pierre Elliott Trudeau from 1972 to 1979 as Solicitor General. I was working for Penthouse Studios doing promotional brochures for Warren's campaign. After the election, Penthouse sent me and another staff member to Ottawa to meet with Warren seeking film or design work for our employer. I had just co-directed a fundraising film for Loyola College in Warren's riding and was anticipating some form of contract work in return for what we had done in his campaign. We chatted about helping him on his campaign in Notre-Dame-de-Grâce suggesting that we scratch his back and he might return the favour. I learned from Warren that just because you are a member of parliament, you can't hand out contracts to companies in your riding and must do a lot of internal lobbying to make things happen. So Warren offered us a drink of Newfoundland Screech, from his desk drawer at 10 am and said have a nice lunch on the hill boys. We thanked him and left his East Block office. I guess that was my first misconception about politics. We never did get any

Federal Liberal Conventions

From 1971-79 I lived in Nova Scotia where I met my friend and Liberal organizer Len Giffen.   He was responsible for rebuilding the Liberal party provincially in the late 1960's. He confided in me and used my company services to further the Provincial Liberal cause, mostly designing and printing campaign material. We made out of province trips together attending Federal Liberal conventions in Ontario as part of the Nova Scotia contingent. Len's job was to oversee the activities of his cabinet minister, and try to keep the minister out of harm's way. Len was the EA (executive assistant) to this minister. Party conventions are held in major hotels that handle 1000 plus delegates from across Canada. The Nova Scotia contingent had hospitality suites for the Premier and cabinet ministers. Sounds wonderful, but when free booze is offered all hell can break loose, and it did. These suites attracted men and women that wanted to associate and have a drink with the people they helped elect. Problem is, the politicians will have a couple of drinks while soaking up the accolades about how great they are, further inflating their enormous egos. Len and myself were in our hotel room at the end of hall, away from the noisy hospitality suite. Soon the open bar was running out of booze and the suite had become a revolving door of young men & women with business cards scripted with room numbers for further reference.

Len had been charged with looking after the liquor which had been shoved under our beds. We knew what was coming from past experience so we locked the booze in the closet of our designated minister's room right next to ours. Shortly afterwards, the minister appeared in the hall thinking the liquor was still under the bed. He entered the room, looked under the bed, looks at us and says, "where is the goddam scotch?" Len rolled his eyes and replied, "It's in your room for safe keeping". Thirty seconds later we heard a loud crash. Len covered his eyes with his hand and muttered, "He didn't ask for the key to the closet.
We'll be paying for that."

At this point Len said he had an appointment with Senator Keith Davey to see if he could get a meeting with the PM to discuss a federal issue in Central Nova. We couldn't get out of the room fast enough. We walked up the hill to meet with Trudeau's Gatekeeper, Keith Davey. His office was tucked away behind a massive wood door in the far corner of the main lobby of the parliament buildings. He greeted us at the door of his office. Len said that he would like to meet with the PM for a few minutes to brief him on Federal issues in Central Nova. Davey replied that it was not possible given the activities around the convention, but he would pass the information along. We thanked him and left satisfied with the meeting and hoped that he would speak to the PM on the issues in Nova Scotia.

**Senator Keith Davey
and Pierre Trudeau**

Not in any hurry to return to the hotel, we headed to Wilfrid's on the Hill for lunch. At lunch I was briefed on the position Keith Davey had in the PM's office. He was the principle secretary to the Prime Minister and also his "Gatekeeper". Mr. Davey has a nickname on the hill, "The Rainmaker". Should anyone cause harm to the PM, Senator Davey will 'rain down on them like the wrath of God'. Likewise, he will be at the door of the PM's office to take the first bullet should an attempt on the PM's life be made. We laughed and Len said, "That's your lesson in **The Game of Politics** for today."

After we finished lunch and rum & cokes we headed back down to our hotel to view the damage. To our surprise, the hall on the 10th floor was quiet and the doors to our adjoining rooms were shut. We looked in the minister's room only to see him flat out on the bed sound asleep. We looked in the closet where the liquor had been stored to find a few 40 pounders of scotch still in the case. Len said he would have to talk to the hotel management about the smashed closet door later. After a short rest in our room, we got ready to go down to the convention floor for the evening to see how the rest of the contingency from Nova Scotia was doing. Just day one in a 3 day party on the Hill.

Working for the Newfoundland Liberal Mafia

The most interesting political event I was involved in with Len Giffen happened in 1974. Joey Smallwood, Newfoundland's premier and the Father of Confederation for Newfoundland was defeated in 1972 after 24 years of being the Liberal premier. He now wanted to run again in 1974. Len and I formed Giffen, Seaton & Associates as the Maritime PR group. We then joined forces with the partnership of Harry Thomas & Laurie Lapierre in Montreal to develop a campaign for him to be re-elected as Premier of Newfoundland and Labrador. Len and I were asked to come to Montreal to meet Joey and his financial backer, John C. Doyle, President of Canadian Javelin Corporation, to talk strategy. What followed is somewhat surreal, but true in **the Game of Politics.** We met in Doyle's office on Sainte-Catherine Street. The office was approximately 40 feet in depth by 20 feet wide with floor to ceiling glass on three sides and a back wall of mahogany panels. We were escorted to the back of the office. John Doyle was at the far end of the room behind one of the biggest carved desks I had ever seen. It probably came from Central America where Javelin operated. Doyle was a big man. He wore a red tie, red pinstriped shirt and large gold cuff links that sparkled in the sunlight and were exposed as he held a large Cuban cigar to his lips. In front of the desk on the right was a mahogany chippendale chair. Joey was perched on it like a falcon ready to swoop down on his prey.

At the far end of the room were three more mahogany chairs placed two feet apart. The three of us were asked to take a seat - Harry Thomas, Len Giffen and me. I had barely put my briefcase down when Joey was on his feet walking back and forth across the rug like a bantam rooster. He turned to look at the three of us and said, "So what are you boys going to do for us?" Doyle took the Cuban out of his mouth and wagged a finger at Joey and said, "Sit down Joe!" When Doyle got up and came around to the front of the desk, we realized just how short Smallwood was. He was about 5 foot 4 inches tall while Doyle was easily over six feet. Addressing all of us, Doyle said, "First we have to get positive media in the Newfoundland papers." Joey exploded out of his chair and started to pace back and forth again, while we sat at the far end of the office, speechless, viewing this circus. Joey stoped and blurted out, "Forget about the St. John Herald, they hate my guts!" Doyle returned to his desk chomping on his Cuban and glared at Joey, "Please sit down Joe, you're scaring the boys." Doyle then said, "So we will just have to buy the fucking newspaper and print what we want. Can you boys handle that?" Harry Thomas, our Montreal partner, spoke up, "I will write press releases for all the papers in Newfoundland, Montreal and Toronto." Harry then introduced Len as being a Liberal organizer and Campaign Manager for two decades. Len would go to Newfoundland and get the message effectively delivered throughout the province. Joey, says, " That's good because on my island

Harry finished the introductions with, "To my right is Win Seaton. He is an expert on all things print and will provide all the marketing materials that are required." The group conversation continued with John Doyle doing most of the talking. He says."Budget…Whatever it costs!" I sort of remember we even had a budget that was submitted by our group the following week that included gifts for campaigning. This is the 1970's but 1930 style campaigning in rural areas of most Canadian provinces still prevailed. The candidate would be driven from one small community to another by his campaign manager who had a trunk full of welcome gifts for a select few leaders in each community, nylon stockings for the women and a bottle of booze for the men. **The Game of Politics"** at its best.

Harry was busy writing press releases about all the things Joe Smallwood had done in his 24 years as Premier, Len was contacting his network of people throughout Newfoundland to see where the support for Joey Smallwood might be for Joey returning as premier.

I was organizing brochure materials and door hangers that were printed up and ready to go, plus padd printing on plastic beer glasses with Joey's picture on them and **"Mr. LIBERAL JOEY".** I remember having several boxes full of these plastic glasses in my Halifax print shop that eventually ended up in the attic of my Milford Station home. They were stored there well into the late 70's.

Joey Smallwood

John C. Doyle

**The front and back panels of a Joey Smallwood
door hanger, printed but never distributed**

Len's inquiries in Newfoundland **turned up where all the bodies were buried.** Meaning the voting public had heard about all the bad stuff Joey was involved in and had no interest or stomach to see Joey Smallwood return as their premier. My guess is that newspapers like the St. John Herald informed the general public about the raping and pillaging. Joey was involved with Hydro Quebec's getting a long term lease on the power produced at Churchill Falls in Labrador/Newfoundland. The 1969 contracts between Hydro/Québec and Hamilton Falls Power Corporation, a private corporation created in 1958 by Brinco. This was one of John Doyle's companies and was partnered with British Newfoundland Corporation that had major investments in Newfoundland and was created by Premier Smallwood in the 1950's. It is inconceivable that any political party today would knowingly and willingly agree to sell its main natural resource for the next 40 to 75 years at a price fixed below the current price. This could only happen if it was forced to do so, or was given commensurate compensation. In this case, the latter did not happen. This outcome ensured that most Newfoundlanders will find it impossible to put the Churchill Falls contract behind them. There has been reams and reams written about this deal and many others, suggesting Joey Smallwood and John Doyle were involved in and received compensation in the Quebec Hydro sell off . Another part of **"The Game of Politics."**

When the pressure from the Law got too much, Doyle escaped to his home in Panama City in Central America. John C. Doyle was the last vestige of Joey Smallwood's industrialization plan for the province of Newfoundland. The Prime Minister at the time, John Diefenbaker, inelegantly put it, "Doyle will end up in the coop for years if he does return to Canada." Joey Smallwood retired to write his memoirs. He died on December 17, 1991, a week before his 91st birthday. John C. Doyle took whatever he could out of the Churchill Falls deal and resettled in Panama City in Panama. He died at home June 1, 2000. He was still a fugitive from Canadian Justice.

After the campaign to re-elect Joey was terminated, I was involved in a few other campaigns in Nova Scotia between 1974 and 1976.

Harry Thomas lived in Montreal where he did PR work for a number of National Companies until his passing from kidney failure in the 1980's.

Len Giffen continued his political career that included serving as a provincial organizer, campaign manager and official agent, executive assistant to ministers in several portfolios and developing training programs for potential workers in all aspects of election campaigns. He left the political sphere when, in his words, "most elected politicians egos quickly grew to the degree that they believed they were elected because they were so smart and brilliant. They didn't need to connect with their constituents anymore concerning political matters and day to day government activity."

Len began to scale back his involvement in political activity in 1974-75 when he accurately predicted that the newly elected Liberal government in Nova Scotia would be defeated in the next election in 1978. This would be in spite of an excellent achievement record. Defeat would be caused by their arrogance. His career continued in the voluntary sector where he ultimately became consultant in volunteer organizational development and was the first Nova Scotian to be elected to the Board of Directors of the International Association of Lions Clubs, the world's largest and most influential service club organization.

In 1979 my printing business was on a downward trend and had not recovered from the six month mail strike of 1976-77. My involvement with the defeated Liberal Party was long gone and it was time to move on. We closed our business, sold our property and resettled in Vancouver B.C. where I had gone to college in the 60's. From 1980 to 83 I returned to the design business. In the fall of '83 to October 1986 I was Design/Marketing Co-ordinator for EXPO '86. I followed up in 1987-89 as Advertising Manager for CVS and Win Seaton Design 1990 to 1999. In May 2000 I retired from running my own design business and teaching at the University College of the Fraser Valley in British Columbia. I re-settled in Nova Scotia again in a small community in North Queen called Kempt, population about 45 souls. I converted an old bakery into an Art Gallery and started painting again. When I joined the North Queens Board of Trade in 2001 there were less than 15 members. By the time I was approached by the Liberals in 2003, I had increased the membership to 65 and brought several small businesses into the fold.

Nomination in Queens County Nova Scotia

Win Seaton

In 2002 I was elected the President of the North Queens Board of Trade. The Conservative government of the day held a meet & greet with Premier John Hamm and his cabinet at the Holiday Inn, downtown Halifax. I was invited along with other Board of Trade presidents from around the province. After that Halifax meeting, the Local Queens Liberal Association asked me if I would let my name stand for candidate nomination in the upcoming provincial election in 2003. I was retired and had been a Liberal all my life. I felt my previous involvement in the 1970's with different campaigns might somehow give me wisdom on how to run my own campaign, but I still had a lot to learn. I had a meeting with the Liberal Association in Liverpool and it was agreed that I would seek the nomination for Queens. I would do my own marketing and media promotion as I had acted in this capacity for other successful Liberals in past Nova Scotia elections. The nomination date was set, and a sitting Liberal member Dr. Jim Smith from Dartmouth-East would run the nomination meeting. I was challenged for the nomination two days before the meeting but that person was unable to get the signature support required.

**John Morse, a Minister in Premier Hamm's Cabinet
in conversation with me at the Board of Trade
Meet & Greet at the Holiday Inn in Halifax**

The week after I was nominated, I received letters of congratulation from Prime Minister Paul Martin; the Chair of the Provincial Liberals, plus a welcome aboard note from Liberal Leader Danny Graham and a phone call from his father Senator Al Graham in Ottawa. I also received a letter from the Mayor of Liverpool John G. Leefe, a former Conservative cabinet minister. In the letter he told me, "Many are those with opinions, much fewer are those who are prepared to put their name on a ballot." My ego was beginning to inflate at the first meeting with the campaign group in Liverpool. That came with a smile and I was telling myself how great I was and things were just getting started. The next ego trip came a few weeks later when Danny Graham and the President of the Nova Scotia Liberals invited all 52 candidates and campaign managers to a Saturday session at a hotel near Truro.

When I walked into the lobby several of the new candidates were bouncing around patting each other on the back like they had just won the lottery. Little did they know about the hard work ahead. Of the 52 candidates at that ego building meeting, the original nine were re-elected and three new candidates won. The other 40 Liberal candidates, including myself, were defeated. This picture is the last ego building event I remember. The group assembled for a photo shoot with Liberal Leader Danny Graham. The photographer wanted Danny to sit in the red leather chair but he declined and someone in the group said put Win in the chair as our "Godfather". If you don't think my ego was bigger than the red chair you're sorely mistaken. As I sat cross legged, my mind was picturing me as the future Minister of Art and Culture in the next government. Ego and Power were in overdrive. I visualized that I would receive more grants for the Art Gallery of Nova Scotia and reverse the budget cuts the Tory government made to Halifax's Neptune Theatre. This is not just a Minister's decision but many others would be involved. The Deputy to the Premier in consultation with the Premier and the senior bureaucrats are the people who finally execute or veto whatever deputy ministers request. Other departmental deputies make their requests to the Premier's deputy. These men and women are lifelong employees of the province. As a senior civil servant put it to me, "Governments come and governments go" but these deputies are career people who have been working all their lives as civil servants.

Left to right seated: Milt Larson, Chester-St. Margaret's, Win Seaton, Queens
Left to right standing: Clifford Huskilson, Shelburne
Danny Graham, Halifax Citadel, John MacDonald, Lunenburg West

QUEENS

At that Saturday ego building session I had a deflating meeting with my Campaign Manager and the Provincial Liberal Campaign Chair from Halifax, referred to in politics as the "Party Bagman." He informed us that he required $5,300 from our campaign funds to promote the leader throughout Nova Scotia This was a shock, and required another rum and coke. I knew the Queens Association only had $1000 in the bank and we were only a week into the campaign. My Campaign Manager said we would look into it and get back to the bagman. In the end he negotiated the amount to $4,000 for the leadership contribution. This output of money forced the Queens Liberals and I to go hat in hand and beg for investment in a Liberal win, not an easy task given the Liberals last win in Queens was some 53 years before. I became the lead "Bagman" along with several dyed-in-the-wool Liberals. We raised $7,565. The local Liberals took out a line of credit with RBC. My family and extended family committed one-third of the campaign which cost almost $22,000. After the election the Association received a provincial rebate of $12,000. from the Liberal Party of Nova Scotia. This amount represented the number of total votes for Queens County. But, we still had to retire the overdraft at RBC, which we did.

<u>Moral of the Story</u>: **Don't even think about politics unless you have disposal income that you won't miss after the election is over.**

One has to have a thick skin and a strong work ethic to go door to door meeting people. It takes stamina. My loss of stamina came in the middle of the campaign while touring a lumber mill in Greenfield Queens. I got an insect bite on my leg that swelled up within an hour. I spent the weekend in the Liverpool Hospital with an IV tube in my arm. I was back door knocking on Tuesday in Broad Cove and Petite Riviera but the three days in hospital took its toll and my energy waned. I retreated back home and prepared for the local TV station three party debate organized by the incumbent MLA Kerry Morash. The NDP candidate Vicki Conrad was better prepared than both Kerry and myself and it showed in the election. She came within a few hundred votes of defeating Kerry and did defeat him in the 2011 election, when the NDP formed the first and only three year government in Nova Scotia. The Liberals were elected in 2014 and still form the government in 2020

L to R: Kerry Marsh - Conservative
Win Seaton - Liberal, Vicki Conrad - NDP

My signs a week before election day

Every campaign has trouble with signage. In my run for office in 2003 the signs took a heavy hit and my sign crew spent many hours replacing them. Fortunately the Association had stored signs from the previous election and all that was needed was an overlay panel with my name overtop of the previous candidate. The Liberal logo was the same as the previous election so we had twice the signage going into the campaign. Queens is a large constituency, sixty kilometers deep by forty-eight wide with several small communities on the Atlantic Ocean. Liverpool was the only large municipality and there was no other core areas for signage. The signage crew put signs on a lot of trees, if only the trees could vote. Newspaper advertising was confined to the local Liverpool paper.

After the August 2003 election was over, Danny Graham was re-elected along with 11 others. Danny led the provincial Liberals for just over a year before stepping down in early 2004 due to his wife's ill health. She had been diagnosed with cancer shortly after her husband won the leadership race in April 2002. The couple had three sons, Patrick, Andrew and Colin. Danny confided in me in late July 2003, when we were campaigning in Liverpool, that his wife's cancer had returned. He really wasn't up to shaking hands so it was no surprise that he resigned on January 12, 2004 to be with his family

**Win Seaton campaigning with Liberal leader
Danny Graham in Liverpool super market**

Leadership Change

Danny Graham's resignation threw the party into leadership mode, and every Liberal in Nova Scotia tried to figure out who to support at the next convention. I and the Queens Liberal team consulted with former two-time Liberal Cabinet Minister in the last Liberal government, Don Downe from Bridgewater. He was at the top of his game in understanding The Game of Politics. He had campaigned with me along the south shore of Queens and Lunenburg counties in 2003. A group of us approached Don but he was lobbying for a Federal Senate seat and declined our offer to support him in a run for the leadership. Five Liberals threw their hats into the ring for the leadership including the re-elected MLA from Annapolis Royal, Steven McNeil. I received a call from Steven asking me if I and the Queens Liberal Association would support him in the Leadership bid, I said I would and would canvas the rest of the organization. It turned out that out of the twelve executive members, seven of us would support Steven and five supported Diana Whalen who represented the electoral district of Halifax Clayton Park. The Leadership convention was held in a Dartmouth rink April 28, 2007. It was a three day affair. I sat in the stands in my Steven McNeil T-shirt, on the front was "All about You" and on the back was "MCNEIL 12". Steven was number 12 of his mothers 17 kids, his mother was Canada's first female sheriff and recipient of the Order of Nova Scotia.

and at the time of the leadership convention, his brother Chris was the Deputy Police Chief in Halifax. During the convention Chris was down on the rink surface working the room. I sat in the stands and had a few words with former Premier Gerald Regan. We talked about his recent heart transplant and I reminded him that we had played pickup hockey together at the Bedford rink a few blocks from his home on Bedford Basin. He commented that we won't be doing that again anytime soon.

Mr. Regan had a long career in politics including several cabinet positions in Pierre Trudeau's governments. After talking to Mr. Regan for a few minutes I went to the coffee shop and sat with Senator Al Graham, Danny's father. I thanked him for his phone call with words of encouragement before my 2003 election run in Queens. He was quite feeble at that point but had to show his Liberal support for his home province of Nova Scotia as did Gearld Regan. I returned to the rink to see more activity on the floor, Scott Brison was working the room for Diana Whalen while his partner Maxine or Max as he is called was approaching the crowd on Steven McNeil's behalf.

I had only met Scott Brison once at Acadia University while attending a reception for the new science building funded by the Irving Family of New Brunswick. He was with Joe Clark who I greatly admired for his foreign policy work on behalf of the Canadian government. Steven McNeil won on the second ballot with 718 votes, Whalen came close with 650 votes.

**Steven McNeil as he appeared
at the leadership convention in Dartmouth 2004**

The Honourable Stephen McNeil Premier of Nova Scotia was first elected to the Nova Scotia House of Assembly as MLA for Annapolis in 2003 and was re-elected in 2006, 2009, 2013 and 2017. Today in November 2019, Steven McNeil has been Premier of Nova Scotia for 6 years and Diana Whalen has retired from Politics.

This leadership event was pretty much my last direct involvement in Liberal politics. I moved back to British Columbia in 2012 and did some work for the Liberal Candidate in my riding of Pitt Meadows/Maple Ridge in the 2015 election and had some minor involvement in this last election in 2019.

The balance of the book is my opinion about the Cardinal Sins committed by the Liberal Party of Canada, senior Cabinet Ministers and Prime Minister Justin Trudeau.

THE CARDINAL SINS
of the Liberal Party in 2019

Jody Wilson Raybould's cardinal sins were against her own Indigenous people and levelled at her Prime Minister, the Principal Secretary & Gatekeeper Gerry Butts and Michael Wernick, Clerk of the Privy Council, as well as Canada's system of democracy that has been used since Confederation in 1867.

A Star is Born

Justin Trudeau, when asked why so many women were appointed to Cabinet, replied "Because its 2015" women have equal rights and should have equal responsibilities in the Government of Canada. This was his rationale for appointing inexperienced members to Cabinet positions in his newly formed government. In past governments, these portfolios had been assigned to senior Members of Parliament, men and women in their second or third terms as MPs. This error by the PM was entirely understandable coming from a newly minted PM who had no real experience in cabinet solidarity or **The Game of Politics.** His short tenure as the sitting member from Papineau in Montreal didn't give him the experience to form a federal cabinet. His name alone was a given in the Liberal Party a few years before and after his second win in Papineau as MP he quickly became the poster boy for the Liberals.

He was quickly elevated to party leader and was seeking to be the next Prime Minister of Canada. Many in the party said he was too inexperienced, but he quickly showed that he inherited the intelligence of his father, grasping issues that ordinary Canadians were concerned about, such as the separation issue in his father's era. After all, the party misfired on the three previous leaders starting with Stephane Dion, Michael Ignatieff and Bob Rae, so how could the party possibly lose with an inexperienced man with the name Trudeau? That was a no brainer.

I heard a CBC Radio discussion that he held in Papineau early in his quest for the top job. The issue was; should "Western Canada separate from Quebec and Canada?" He brought a representative group from Alberta and the Prairies to meet with him on his home turf in Papineau, to present their views on separation. Justin explained in the most eloquent way that this was not an option for them and Canada. It was the most intelligent conversation I had ever heard from a politician.

The CBC listeners across Canada realized that he had more to offer in debating issues than his father, whose vocabulary often consisted of a one finger silent salute or simply saying, "Fuddle Duddle." From those early interviews, Justin planted the seed in the media that he was not his father but his own man and a new way of seeing the future must be his goal for the people of Canada.

Pierre's infamous pirouette behind the Queen

Besides inheriting his father's intelligence, he also inherited his parents' flare for drama. In Pierre's case it was doing a pirouette behind the Queen, in Justin's case it was getting into a boxing ring with a Conservative Indigenous MP that had a huge weight advantage and beating the living crap out of him. He also had his mother's genes and flare in other ways. Margaret, the flower girl love child, gave her son his handsome looks and that wavy black hair and Kennedy swagger. But the most important thing she gave to her son was survival over everything including **The Game of Politics.**

Trudeau Mania

Trudeau Mania started again in the early months of 2015 after being in the closet for 47 years. I had personally experienced it in Montreal in 1968. The official **Trudeau Mania** started at the Liberal convention on April 3, 1968, in Toronto. Pierre Elliot Trudeau's charismatic display on the convention floor emerged when he was elected as party leader and ran for Prime Minister in the federal election held two months later on June 25, 1968.

Justin's first cardinal sin, from my point of view, came with the inexperienced Justin Trudeau appointing first time elected MPs to senior cabinet portfolios. This happened for a few different reasons. Trudeau's belief that women have equal rights and should have equal responsibilities in the government of Canada. He did not understand the responsibility of these senior portfolios since he never held a cabinet portfolio and was only appointed as a critic in the House of Commons.

Justin did not understand the culture of groups or organizations that have both male and female members such as the RCMP or Canadian Armed Forces. I am referring to an existing culture of harassment, verbal or negative body language and bullying. As the former Commissioner of the Royal Canadian Mounted Police, Bob Paulson, put it when asked why so many women in the RCMP filed harassment complaints against their fellow male members, Paulson replied, "Men and women are wired differently." Initially this appeared to be Justin Trudeau's main cause of misunderstanding with Jody Wilson Raybould's reaction of interference in the SNC-Lavalin story. The cause was far more than simply getting her wires crossed with the Prime Minister's. She saw the SNC-Lavalin issue as illegal and political interference from the Prime Minister. He saw it as just another thing that needed solving. In Jody's statement, "She was trying to protect the PM from himself," and asked the Clerk of the Privy Council if he fully understood the ramifications on him and the party if this became public. Obviously, she didn't understand anything about governing Canada and precious little about the Laws of the land regarding the way **The Game of Politics** is played.

In October 2015, the new Liberal MPs arrived in Ottawa with inflated egos, ignited by their unexpected wins and not prepared to accept the fact that the only reason they were there was because they won on the coat tails of Justin Trudeau. I remember in July 1968, when Pierre Trudeau won the election, looking at the new crop of MPs that were first elected and was heard to say, "They were just a whole bunch of nobodies." That was then and this is now, or is it? The arrogance and egos are the same. Instant gratification with the son's rise to fame came quick and fast with thousands of "selfies" that gave instant gratification from young and old. Justin's new crop of MPs mostly came from ordinary backgrounds with ordinary incomes and ordinary jobs. Very few were famous people or astronauts. By the end of the first month in Ottawa the new 'nobodies' were dead tired from all the briefings. This deflated some egos that thought they were the chosen ones to run the country and create more jobs and bring federal funds to their constituency. MPs salaries, on the most part, are three times that of the yearly income most were making back home. A few of them were appointed to special committees while others were appointed to Cabinet. The ego goes into over-drive and the head inflates to exploding proportions. They thought they would be responsible for running the government of Canada. This is where the Liberal Party commits a major Cardinal Sin by not telling the new MPs the naked truth.

Prime Ministers and Cabinet Ministers do not run the Government of Canada. The permanent Public Service assists in the administration of the government, implements policy, delivers programs, and provides advice to the Cabinet. These Four Institutions called **"Central"** run the Government of Canada; the **Privy Council Office**, the **Treasury Board Secretariat**, the **Cabinet**, and the **Department of Finance.**

The Liberal Party of Canada doesn't include an entry level class in **"The Game of Politics - 101"** to explain to the newly elected MPs how the above Institutions run the Government of Canada. The fact is, there are no written rules and the only way any new MP learns about the game of politics is to participate and learn on the job. If you are a quick learner and have street smarts you might just survive, many do not like Jody Wilson Raybould.

Public servants are non-partisan and serve the government, regardless of which party is in power. The Privy Council Office is the Prime Minister's government department. It is staffed by public servants and by the Clerk of the Privy Council who is also secretary to the Cabinet and de facto head of the public service. The (PCO) co-ordinates the activities of the government and oversees the appointment of senior officials in departments, agencies, and crown corporations. It provides non-partisan advice and administrative support to the Prime Minister and the Cabinet.

Cardinal Sins committed by Jody Wilson Raybould

Jody Wilson Raybould

First Sin of her many sins started when she was moved from Minister of Justice & Attorney General and refused to take on the Indigenous Services portfolio that Trudeau offered her. She said "I have spent my life opposed to the Indian Act of 1867 and couldn't be in charge of the programs administered under its authority" even with the PM's explanation that he was concerned over maintaining the reconciliation momentum and needed her leadership within the Indigenous community. This was an incredible statement coming out of her mouth considering she has helped to build bridges between the First Nations communities and the Canadian government while committed to helping Indigenous peoples seek self-government and gain equality in education, health care and legal rights. She started as Provincial Crown Prosecutor in Vancouver's downtown Eastside and strove to reduce that area's high rate of incarceration of Indigenous residents seeking to address their marginalization, poverty and inequality.

Second Sin was when the Prime Minister offers you a portfolio in his Cabinet, you don't refuse to accept it, no matter what your personal emotions are telling you.

Jody's response to that was, "I am a former BC crown prosecutor doing a good job in the Justice portfolio, I am a lawyer that believes in doing things by the letter of the law." She should have sucked it up, accepted the challenge and looked for future opportunities. In a matter of one minute of anger and frustration, she destroyed all the hard work she had done relating to her own Indigenous people to say nothing about Bills C-14, C-16, C-45, C-78 that she lobbied for and helped make into law. She knows, as all politicians know, very few bills are passed unless you are in a majority sitting government. The disservice she has done to her own Indigenous people by turning a blind eye to all the issues and things her government had promised to do for reconciliation. If she believed her government's mandate was to move forward with reconciliation, she would have been in the best position to table private member's bills to make changes to the Indian Act of 1867. Now, the possibility is gone and Jody Wilson Raybould is left with her over heated emotions that she did the right thing by not accepting this portfolio and then resigned.

Third Sin occurred when Jane Philpott, Minister of Indigenous Services, was asked to take over the cabinet position as Head of the Treasury Board to replace the retiring Scott Brison. Shortly after she was sworn in as Head of the Treasury Board, she resigned in support of Jody's decision and the Prime Minister's handling of the Cabinet shuffle.

Fourth Sin was when Jody Wilson Raybould departed from Cabinet followed by reports that the Prime Minister's Office had pressured her to intervene in a federal case against SNC-Lavalin, directing federal prosecutors to negotiate a deal with the company. It was public knowledge that the Quebec company had been charged in 2013 with bribing Libyan officials in exchange for construction contracts. The national media published an unnamed source that said that Wilson Raybould had refused this directive, which would have led to SNC-Lavalin receiving a fine in a deferred prosecution agreement instead of facing a criminal trial. In the Justice Committee presentation on February 27, 2019, probing Jody Wilson Raybould, she affirmed that she had tried to stop "consistent and sustained" political interference from the Prime Minister's Office in this matter, citing prosecutorial independence as one of her core values. She said she felt that her stance on this issue had resulted in her removal from the Department of Justice. She was totally correct in assuming that she was removed from the Justice portfolio for playing lawyer on the SNC-Lavalin deferred prosecution agreement.

She has no one to blame for her fall from grace. She failed to understand "It's all about the Economy Stupid." SNC-Lavalin is a major player in the Canadian economy as one of the top 100 public sector companies that have infrastructure projects under development across Canada worth over $200 billion.

SNC-Lavalin currently employs 9,000 people in Quebec, including about 700 at its head office in Montreal. More than half of its Canadian employees work outside Quebec. Many are currently engaged in multibillion dollar projects across Canada that won't be finished for several years. Again Jody did not have any knowledge of the construction industry. SNC-Lavalin has several projects ongoing across the country and if they were stopped from bidding for 10 years, many of these projects would sit unfinished for years, because most construction projects are based on a quote Cost-Plus system. Most of these big projects are subject to additional costs that can't be foreseen, such as acts of God, floods, earthquakes, or escalating material costs. In Jody's own front yard at her constituency office on Broadway & Granville in Vancouver, SNC-Lavalin could have contracts to extend Vancouver's sky train system which could require cost-plus quoting. The whole economy of Canada has to be supported by the government of the day. It's really inconceivable that Jody could not fathom the fact that her government has a standing policy. If a major company needs help and is part of Canada's economic growth, the government doesn't hesitate in providing what is required to move it forward. Recent corporations that received this help included Bombardier, General Motors, and the pipelines. Jody Wilson-Raybould doesn't understand the **"The Game of Politics."**

Gerry Butts and Justin Trudeau

Fifth Sin: When she called out Gerry Butts, Principal Secretary & Gatekeeper to the PM. Not only did she not understand or care that he is the most important person and confidant to Trudeau. Gerry Butts is the PM's Gatekeeper and his job means that everything and every person must go through him to the Prime Minister. He oversees the PM's Office and is in on all conversations of substance with the PM. He also sits in cabinet as the PM's second set of eyes and ears. His job is to protect the PM from harm at all costs. If the PM's office staff or the PM are threatened by individual persons or other parties, the gatekeeper must fall on his sword and take the blame for the PM and resign. This is another accepted rule of **"The Game of Politics"**. Jody has hurt the reputation of the PM but he will recover and move on while Mr. Butts career could be on hold until the election in October.

Jody suggested that Mr. Butts was the main reason for miscommunication between herself and the PM and stated, "Doesn't he understand the damage to him and the party if the SNC-Lavalin deal goes through?" In other words, 'pay to play' a fine for their bribery program in another country, at another time and allowing them to quote on Canadian government contracts. This came out of her mouth at the tribunal when she spilled her guts about Gerry Butts involvement thus opening the door for the whole world to view. From this point on Jody Wilson Raybould had no way back and no future in Federal politics. She and Jane Philpott will get media attention for a while but in a few months they will fade into the woodwork and election issues of the day will be the news. We live in a world of instant gratification.

Justin Trudeau and Michael Wernick

Sixth Cardinal Sin was Jody's lack of understanding that Cabinet Ministers and Prime Ministers do not run the Government of Canada. The Clerk of the Privy Council and other deputies control all aspects of the government. Ministers can go to their designated Deputy with a request to do something but there is no assurance that the minister will get any satisfaction. If budgets are involved, the Deputy Minister of Finance will meet with the Clerk of the Privy Council and they will decide. In the end, all MPs and the Cabinet are elected and are not employees. The Deputies are career public servants and most are 30 year plus government employees. This system was adopted from Great Britain where the privy council served to advise the Monarch, Prime Ministers and ministers of government for centuries. Canada has used the system since Confederation in 1867. In Canada, the Clerk of the Privy Council holds three positions. The first is to act as the Deputy Minister to the Prime Minister. The second is to be Secretary to the Federal Cabinet and the third is to act as the Head of the Federal Public Service. In other words the "Top Dog in the Federal Government." When Jody appeared before the Justice Committee, she attacked the trust that resides with the Clerk's office stating the pressure put on her from the Clerk was political interference and illegal. This was something that had never been done before. She forced Michael Wernick to appear before the Justice Committee and explain that there was nothing illegal about the SNC-Lavalin issue. This was part of his job as the PM's Deputy Minister.

This is an effective way for the clerk to make sure that ministers have the facts because they also want good decision making. He wants everything on the table for ministers to take into account.

Wernick went on to explain to the Justice Committee that he had performed these services for the previous governments of Brian Mulroney, Jean Chrétien and Paul Martin and that they were satisfied with his work. It was all above board and legal and that his office had been trusted for decades. Jody Wilson-Raybodt was naive to think that she could make changes to the core way the democratic Government of Canada had functioned since Confederation.

On a morning radio show, April 24, 2019, Jody was telling a group of Indigenous People the government is still trying to back out of their promised commitments to the Indigenous people that was promised in 2015. Had she accepted the portfolio containing the Indian Act of 1867, she could have influenced changes to the Act to reverse the way indigenous people have been treated by the federal government since Confederation. She now has zero influence and is on the outside looking in. **This is her greatest Sin, committed against her own indigenous people.**

She should have stopped at giving her testimony to the Justice Committee, let Mr. Butts and Mr. Wernick explain their views on conversations about SNC-Lavalin, and stated that there was no illegal activity in pursuing the whole issue.

But she brought the clerk back to testify a second time to explain his function as a trusted employee for all governments. She then promptly produced the audio tape conversation she had had with the clerk and secretly recorded. He shortly afterward resigned saying the trust he had with this government was broken and he no longer could do his job. Before she made the audio tape public there was some chance of forgiveness but this was the final Cardinal Sin, if Canada was a third world country she would have gone before a firing squad. It never even occurred to her the long term sin she had inflicted on the present government and future governments with the lack of trust with every ministers designated deputy. The new Clerk of the Privy Council Ian Shugart replaced Michael Wernick before the seat was cold. Mr. Shugart will not quickly forget it was a Conservative Justice Committee that pushed his predecessor on the SNC-Lavalin issue and ultimately caused him to resign. This is a serious blow to our system of government. The Deputies are in a position to stonewall anything a Minister of the Crown requests. If the former Minister, Jody Wilson Raybolt asked her deputy for something, he or she can say, "that's not available." Jody then could say "I will have you fired". The next morning she would get a call from the Public Service Union telling her "No Can Do".

I once heard a Deputy Minister say, **"I am a lifer the Minister will be gone in a year or two".**

Jody Wilson Raybould's whole attitude was her driving ambition to first be a lawyer and secondly to become Prime Minister. A noble ambition for an aboriginal woman and a lawyer, but with all this ambition she forgot to play "**The Game of Politics**". **B**eing naive is one thing; learning to work the system is another thing. She did neither. Early reports in 2016 with Liberals in Vancouver, quickly showed she was not a team player. With her virtues of honesty, loyalty, her aim to do the right thing, she has systematically written a whole new manual on how to get fired in politics. Even today when she is no longer in Cabinet, in Caucus, or in the Party, she still talks about the public wanting honesty and truth in their politicians. She insists that when the government promises the Indigenous Peoples something like clean water and housing, they should deliver. Her problem is these things are being done but not on her time line. She is the first and only Indigenous woman that could have pushed the reconciliation with the native peoples of Canada that is long overdue. **She Blew it**. She didn't understand how our political system in Canada works. We are a Capitalist Society based on Money and Power both of which presently reside with the Federal Liberal Government. If, for one moment, she thought she could change this fact, she is more than naive she is just plain stupid. But this author will predict the Liberals and their leader will slow down on reconciliation and quietly push it to the back burner after the 2019 election. The minority government will have more pressing issues like the economy, jobs, pipe lines and environmental issues. Justin Trudeau will have to back track on all the "Sunny Days" he promised in 2015 and be more accountable to the Canadian public.

Jody Willson Raybolt will fade from politics. As an Independent Member of Parliament, she will become a non-entity for any government agency, provincial, federal or municipal. One cannot call or suggest your boss is untruthful or a liar and survive in Politics or any other job. Jody's win in Vancouver/Granville will give her a back row seat in the House, but nothing else. The Speakers of the House, will not allow JWR the privilege of rising in the House to speak. Most Canadians in Canada have watched government after government, for decades, give the Indigenous Peoples billions of dollars only to see it disappear with. nothing to show for it. The native people in Canada make up one of the largest government-dependent groups in the World. Now they have lost their **"Joan of Arc"**

Jody's father, an Indigenous Chief on Vancouver Island, stated his daughter was a strong woman and would someday become Prime Minister of Canada. To be elected as Prime Minister of Canada you have to be leader of a national party. Jody doesn't have one and never will.

Dr. Jane Phillpot was not re-elected as an Independent in Markham North. she had wanted to hold the government accountable for their actions and stated that the Liberals had some very good programs but she wanted to represent the people of Markham without party interference. On the other hand, Jody Wilson Raybould's independent candidate speech looked and sounded like the launch of a new National Indigenous Party. Her only reference to a party was an Independent Indigenous logo banner beside her with clear Indigenous graphics that suggest to me she will move to start her own Indigenous Party. On August 20 while campaigning in Vancouver/ Granville she said, " I didn't see myself as part of any federal party ".

I am like a square peg in a round hole" I'm not a political party person." She also said, that the federal Liberals will keep the money her Electoral District Association raised over the three and half years she was the elected a Member of Parliament.

End Game in the SNC-Lavalin affair

In late December 2019 the courts solved the whole issue. The guilty executives were prosecuted on bribery and fraud charges with a few executives going to jail for related contracts with Libya. SNC-Lavelin agreed to pay a $280-million penalty fine which is what the Liberals always wanted. Other charges, including those against the parent company, were stayed, meaning SNC-Lavalin Construction was allowed to quote on all their cost plus projects and future contracts in Canada.

The Liberal government and the Prime Minister got to retain the 9,000 jobs in Quebec but The Liberal government has to accept the damaging way the PM and others handled the whole affair. Justin Trudeau can repeat "His job is to retain jobs and create new jobs." Jody will fade into the woodwork, but her sins toward the Liberal Party of Canada & Clerk of the Privy Council will not soon be forgotten. When the verdict came down on Dec. 19th, Jody issued this statement:

"The report represented vindication for the independence of the role of attorney general and director of public prosecutions and validated critical concerns raised by her, but also said she felt "sadness" seeing how the affair has played out. "In a country as great as Canada, essential values and principles that are the foundation for our freedoms and system of government should be actively upheld by all, especially those in positions of public trust."

The Victory Fund and other donations to the association will be going to the next Liberal candidate's campaign. She also said only a few colleagues within the Liberal caucus have communicated with her.

This author suggests all her sins toward the Liberal Party, the Prime Minister and the Government of Canada have finally sunk in and her future in politics, if any, will be extremely limited. Liberals appointed long time Cabinet Minister Carolyn Bennett to be the Minister of Crown–Indigenous Relations. This suggests that the PM wants the whole thing on reconciliation to slow down, under her faithful direction. Jody's departure from the Liberal Party gave the Liberal establishment a breather but they recognized the damage done by the SNC-Lavalin scandal. It was a hard pill to swallow but the Liberals thought they were home free and moving towards winning the election.

Not so! A few weeks before the election the **Grave Diggers** dug up a body that was buried for eighteen years. A black and white photograph of **Justin Trudeau in Brown Face appeared on the National news.**

The PM had committed the most damaging Cardinal Sin to himself and the Liberal Party of Canada. He was being called out for something he did 18 years ago. He wore a costume dressed as "Aladdin" with a turban and brown face make-up. The only way this could be more damaging to the Prime Minister and the Party is if he had had an affair with one of the four women in the photograph. As a visual artist, I have always believed "One Good Picture is worth a Thousand Words." So when the world was shown that one good picture of Justin's "Brown Face", by the media investigators or **"Grave Diggers"**within minutes the talking heads declared "He must be a racist". I will not lower myself to write pages of dribble about this perceived sin as Justin said himself, "I should have known better". But, really, did he think 18 years ago he would be in politics and filling his fathers shoes. I really don't think so.

He was a Drama teacher, in a private school in Vancouver, **get it folks….. A Drama Teacher.**

This error in judgement was entirely understandable considering his early adult life had no politics in it. There was no reason to hide any of his personal life. Andrew Scheer used a rather dull knife to do a little blood letting stating **"This man is not fit to be Prime Minister."**

While Jagmeet Singh decided he would do a more heartfelt act of disbelief with a hint of a tear. Jagmeet looked sincere but then again he also was in Quebec trying to hold onto the 14 NDP seats he had in the province.

This perceived sin by Justin might have the party faithful saying, "I told you so, he was too young and inexperienced and now we are going to loose the election.

But, by this time, weeks before the election, The Big Red Machine had rolled across Canada from coast to coast. The neigh-sayers had forgotten why they had voted him in as party leader.

From the first chapter, after all the party misfired on the three previous leaders starting with Stephane Dion, Michael Ignatieff and Bob Rae, so how could the party possibly lose with an inexperienced man with the name Trudeau? That was a given and a "No Brainer."

This explains who Justin Trudeau really is. Yes, he is from a privileged background with little exposure to racism of any kind, but he is way more than that. He has all the appeal of a Kennedy plus other worldly skills that none of the other federal leaders have or will have as we move forward into 2020 and beyond.

Political Fallout after October 21

After the election, many Liberal MPs openly expressed the thought that the"Brown Face" photo had cost them another majority government. Maybe, but highly unlikely. It was more to do with **"once a Conservative always a Conservative."** Harper was gone. It was time to return to the fold. Most swing ridings, swung back. The changes were made. But the plans were in place to ensure that officials and Ministers of the Crown like Jody Wilson Raybold never again have access to Canada's Democratic System. The mistakes in appointing ministers purely on gender were corrected and the new flock of ministers are now appointed on talent and loyalty to the PM and party. A lot I have written about is pretty negative, but it's the only democratic system we have and like our antiquated laws, things have to change. I think we are moving in the right direction with a minority Liberal government and a modern day leader within the NDP that will work toward environmental issues and sustain our economic growth that is the engine to fight climate change. The majority of Canadians don't understand that you can't have climate control development without economic stability in this country. Canada only has Natural Resources to sell to the rest of the world. If Canada doesn't sell our resources to other countries, we could become a third world country in a next few decades.

Resources we have that most Countries don't have but want are Oil, Natural Gas, Wheat, Wood Products, Water, Iron Ore, Science and Space Development. The minority Liberal government will have to get support from the other parties to move things ahead. It's quite obvious the election shows how divided the Canadian public is when it comes to politics. The mistrust in the general public's view of politicians has never been greater. The general consensus is "Politicians are Takers and not Givers; Liars; Ego-driven; Power Hungry; and spend the peoples money like water flowing out of a tap." As an observer of politics and participant for some **50+** years, I agree there is a great deal of truth to these perceptions.

The election results show the Cardinal Sins started not just in 2019 but soon after Justin Trudeau took office in 2015. His pronouncements of "Sunny Ways Ahead" and "It's 2015" and the Cabinet will be made-up of half woman can be considered a positive gesture, but as I have written about the SNC-Lavalin issue that came back to bite the Liberals and PM in 2019. Other early Cardinal Sins by the PM were traveling the world and not paying enough attention to the promises he made to the Canadian people. He became star struck with all the attention and fixated on repairing the damage Steven Harper had done to foreign affairs. But the PM appears to be a slow learner because he is off again seeking a seat on the UN Security Council.

Politics is a very perceived thing with the population, so when the PM bought a pipeline for 4.6 billion dollars, the population said there he goes again spending the peoples money, a perceived sin. The Environmentalists viewed it as just another attempt by the Federal Government to appease the western oil industry, and get ahead of the court rulings by the Indigenous Peoples to pass over their lands.

Two weeks before the election Mrs. Trudeau stood in front of me and my local PM and stated "The Liberals are not in the business of owning a pipeline." So I have to believe this was another sin by the PM in jumping the queue. The election has also revealed other short comings of a Majority Liberal Government. The alienation of Western Canada has come back with Liberal losses from 2015 and a stronger Conservative representation now heading to Ottawa, with no expectations of getting any partnership project moneys. In my own riding here in BC the Liberal lost the seat to a Conservative that can do nothing for this western community being a non-government MP.

Major infrastructure projects in my riding will stop for the next few years. Overpasses, Highway Projects, Recreational Complexes, etc. Most Canadians do not understand that all major infrastructure projects only happen with the help of the "PARTNERSHIP" system Municipal ,City, Provincial and Federal moneys.

After the PM's attempt failed to bring the provinces on board on the carbon tax he lost status with five provincial Premiers. This is a problem all PMs have had for decades so we can't call this a personal sin. Today, after the election the PM has stated he understands Western concerns and will work hard with the minority parties and strive to make things better for the country as a whole. When asked about a coalition I sensed his father's one finger salute and then the PM softly said, "**No**".

In Justin Trudeau's 2015 campaign promise to change the electoral system. This idea was quickly dropped when he got to caucus and the Liberal brain trust in Ottawa where he was told **"No Way Jose"**

This was just another example of his inexperience. One of the downsides of a proportional system is that they almost always end in coalition governments and no one party gets a majority and has a mandate to govern. Typically, this means less is accomplished as the ruling government has to compromise and negotiate on everything which slows the process down.

First Past the Post

only works in a Horse Race

If the Liberals and Justin Trudeau had committed to this proportional voting system this would have been his ultimate Cardinal Sin and Liberals would have lost the Canadian election in 2019

Here are the results from a November 15, 2019 Breakdown:

With this type of electoral system, the **Liberals** would go from 157 seats to 112 seats and the **Conservatives**, from 121 to 117. In this case, Andrew Scheer's party would be in the lead.

The **NDP** would have more than doubled its number of seats, from 24 to 54. The **Bloc Québécois** would have elected fewer MPs, with 26, instead of 32.

As for the **Green Party**, they would have elected seven times the number of MPs (22 instead of 3). The **People's Party** would have 6 MPs in the House of Commons instead of none.

Candidates are voted for once in their riding with another vote for the party. Constituency MPs are elected in the same way they are now. The remaining seats are proportionally allocated according to the number of votes for each party across the country. For these proportional seats, MPs are elected from lists drawn up by the parties.

With this type of system **(used in Japan),**

The **Liberals** would have formed a minority government, but with 142 seats instead of 157.

The **Conservatives** would have won 120 seats instead of 121.

The **Bloc Québécois** would have approximately the same number of elected MPs (30 instead of 32) and the

New Democrats would have made important gains, with 34 seats instead of 24.

The **Green Party** would have elected 6 additional MPs and the **People's Party** would have made its entry into the House of Commons with 2 MPs.

Another alternative is the mixed-member compensatory system, used in **Germany** and recommended for Canada by the House of Commons Special Committee on Electoral Reform in 2016. Voters get two ballots: one for a riding MP and one for the party. Compensatory seats are awarded according to the proportion of votes at the regional or provincial level. A party who wins 10 per cent of the votes, but doesn't elect an MP, would obtain enough seats to attain 10 per cent representation in Parliament. Those MPs are elected from party lists and represent regional or provincial boundaries.

**With this voting system, that better reflects the popular vote, as well as regional specificities,
The Conservatives would have 117 elected MPs (instead of 121). The Liberals would have 112 seats, a 44-seat loss.**

But the NDP would have benefited the most, with 30 more seats (54 instead of 24). The Bloc would have 26 seats, instead of 32.

This type of electoral system would also have been very advantageous for the Greens (22 seats instead of 3) and the People's Party (6 seats instead of none)

The introduction of a different voting system has been floated on a number of occasions in Canada - notably in British Columbia, Ontario and Prince Edward Island - but without any success. The changes were rejected during referendums. In Quebec, the CAQ government promises to hold a referendum on electoral reform in the next general election in 2022. Now that Canadians have elected a minority government, will the Liberals be influenced by the NDP and the Greens, who both have called for electoral reform?

Methodology

We used the results of the 2019 general election (last update: Oct. 22 at 6:10 a.m. ET) and kept only the parties with more than 0.3 per cent of the popular vote, which corresponds to one seat in a proportional voting system. For the purposes of this simulation, we excluded independent MP Jody Wilson-Raybould.

We drew on the 2016 report of the House of Commons Special Committee on Electoral Reform, which recommends that two-thirds of MPs be directly elected to constituencies and one-third be elected from party lists. These proportions would therefore correspond to 226 riding seats and 112 list (or compensatory) seats. However, our calculations are an approximation. We must consider the fact that with a different voting system, party strategies and voter behaviour would likely differ.

Mélanie Meloche-Holubowski — reporter; Nael Shiab — data journalist; Melanie Julien — desk editor; Francis Lamontagne — designer.

Glossary

Terms used in Canadian Politics

Knows where the Bodies are Buried: This wording refers to a long time party member who has participated in several elections and knows the history of the party, and individual backgrounds party members that they want buried and forgotten that the public doesn't need to know about.

Grave Digger: people that work for the opposition parties that check files, old newspaper articles, employment background checks, court appearances, fines, divorces, child welfare abuses, etc. Ex: Justin Trudeau's Black Face

Vetting: Checking potential candidates' backgrounds to see if the party organizers want a given person to represent the party in an election.

Reason for Vetting: Political parties have difficulty getting professional people like Lawyers, Doctors, Business Leaders to leave their chosen professions and seek public office. So Vetting is used to find the best available person to represent the party.

Green lighting: party sign off on candidate nomination papers

Bagman: Person or persons that collect campaign funds, from companies or well-heeled individuals to fund campaigns.

Political Hack: party follower that turn up every election to advise the candidate with unwanted advice on how to do this or that from years of experience watching, but not doing.

Talking Heads: The media people on TV and Radio that analyze the politicians and their every move, with very little research and less knowledge, providing their own opinions, not facts.

Glossary Continued...

Terms used in Canadian politic

Gatekeeper: Person that has many job titles. Personal secretary to a minister or prime minister, Chief advisor, Personal protector from any form of negative action against said Minister and quite often runs the Minister's office.

Cigar Tube: If a MP or MLA is not within driving distance to their respective legislature and have to fly back and forth on a plane (Cigar Tube) example: a Federal MP on the East Coast or West Coast will fly back and forth on a weekly basis to their constituency. They think they are living in a Cigar Tube.
If you're an MP from Vancouver after the house breaks on Thursday you catch the red eye for Vancouver arriving after midnight, then its up early Friday into the office for meetings with local issues all day. Friday evening dinner meeting with business people or other local politicians. All day Saturday visiting and talking to constituency groups. Sunday afternoon back to the airport arriving back in Ottawa around midnight on a cigar tube.

Working the Room: This term is usually used in conventions when senior party representatives move through a crowded group of card carrying party members trying get individuals to vote for whomever they are supporting. The most common situation is a leadership convention.

Blood Letting: Severely criticizing members of the opposition parties publicly or in the press.

Pay to Play: The SNC-Lavalin was to pay the fine that the court levelled on them and they would be allowed to continue playing The Game of Politics and quote on future federal government contracts across Canada.

As closing thoughts creep into my fingers:

My early writing on page 32 about my explanation of a sin by the federal party as a whole, saying if they had an entry level program for new MPs arriving in Ottawa the first time in **The Game of Politics 101.** Maybe we wouldn't have a Jody Wilson Raybolt trying to bring down our democratic government and our Prime Minister if such a program existed.

It would be my wish that the minister of education or other MPs would but forward a private members bill to create a **"The Game of Politics-101"** course for new MPs, and the government put into law that all Senior Secondary Schools in Canada must have a compulsory course as they reach the voting age, instructed by their local MP.

My former Local Liberal MP confirmed his arrival in Ottawa in October 2015 was met with total lack of organization by the National Liberal Party and no constructive directions on how these new MPs should function or play **The Game of Politics.** He was one of the few new MPs that had street smarts and was quick to seek out and head up a federal committee. He understood the problem given his former career in training people in the food industry. But true to form the National Liberals stonewalled his proposal to implement a course in **The Game of Politics**

The Publisher's logotype is copyrighted

The Young Teazer was an American Schooner that preyed on the sea trade of the British Empire off the coast of Nova Scotia. The Young Teaser, was being chased by British Ships, escaped into the fog, later to be pursued in **Mahone Bay.** As a boarding party prepared to board her, the Young Teazer exploded killing all but 8 crew members. Legend has it that on the anniversary of the sinking of the **Young Teazer,** on a foggy night within 3 days of a full moon, one can witness the appearance of the phantom ship sailing into Mahone Bay only to vanish as"a flaming wreck into the fog".

National Library of Canada Cataloging in Publication Teazer Publishing-ISBN 978-0-9876720-0-1-10